What People Are Saying About
The Collaborator Rules

"Sally's indispensible book is fun, easy to read and loaded with essential information. Don't even think about collaborating without reading it!"

Mark Steisel
ghostwriter

"I received from this delightful book many nuggets of wisdom that will help me be a more effective collaborator. Sally combines a light-hearted, humorous and entertaining style with very, very important lessons If you are thinking of collaborating, are in the midst of doing so, or have done so previously, I suggest you read this book."

Bob Burg
author of *Endless Referrals* and co-author of *The Go-Giver*

"Laced with humor, Shields has a knack for tackling the most sensitive of topics head-on, but with wit and grace. You will laugh out loud while potentially saving yourself much unnecessary contention. *The Collaborator Rules* rule!"

John Curtis, Ph.D.

"As a co-author of numerous projects, I can say from experience that collaboration can be daunting and disappointing. *The Collaborator Rules* gives us sound advice. Follow the rules and don't be afraid to say "No!" It's a great book and I recommend it to any author or collaborator."

Douglas E. Noll
radio host and founder of, *nollassociates.com*

"Handy rules that will save us all a lot of stress & trouble... *The Collaborator Rules* book is a keeper!!"

Jim Agnew
reviewer, producer and literary researcher

"The Collaborator Rules is funny, insightful and full of great tips to make your next collaboration both a successful and fun endeavor."

Dr. Joe Rubino
founder and CEO, *CenterForPersonalReinvention.com*

"Writing is personal, intimate and emotional, and Sally knows the importance of rules in relationships. Her "Daughter-In-Law Rules" will keep families together for generations, and now she's done the same for authors, editors and creative writers who want to work together. Don't even think about collaborating on your next project without first reading "Collaborator Rules!"

Jim Buchard
speaker and author, *Dynamic Components of Personal Power*

"*The Collaborator Rules* offers wise and upbeat advice. Sally Shields practices what she preaches, while passing on her life lessons in a fun, compelling, and caring way."

LeslieBeth Wish, Ed.D.
psychologist, social worker and author

"I've been a partner in sixteen bestselling collaborations and I wish I'd had this book from the start. *The Collaborator Rules* is joyful, easy reading and hugely informative. Collaboration begins and ends well with fail-safe rules and author Sally Shields has covered it all. Trust her!"

Sherry Suib Cohen
collaborator with Star Jones, Estee Lauder
among many others

"With delightful simplicity and humor, *The Collaborator Rules* hands us step-by-step guidelines to happy working partnerships. I only wish I had access to this information years ago!"

Shoshana Bennett, Ph.D.
international speaker, trainer and author of,
Postpartum Depression For Dummies

"Before considering a collaborator for any written work, you absolutely MUST read *The Collaborator Rules*! This fast, but important read by Sally Shields will guarantee your writing bliss and save you from costly missteps along the way. You've already learned the 'who-what-where' of writing; Sally will teach you 'when-why-what for' of collaboration."

Jamie Saloff
author, book consultant and designer

"Rather than overload pages with self-help-speak, Shields keeps her points short and funny. Pick any page and you'll find a smart tip and a chuckle."

Dave Lefkowitz
radio host and founder, *TotalTheater.com*

"Outstanding! Sally Shields has written the manual for life in the guise of a handbook for writers."

Kurek Ashley
international bestselling author, speaker, peak performance coach

"Easy, lighthearted, brilliant! The Collaborator Rules is an easy to read manual for ALL human relationships. I couldn't put it down!"

Lou Kelly
radio host

"In *The Collaborator Rules*, Sally Shields cleverly intertwines subliminal life lessons between the lines of this narrative in a light and easy to read format."

Rick Frishman
founder, *planned television arts*

"Sally Shields thoroughly covers every aspect of partnership enabling a team to prepare for the publication process. *The Collaborator Rules* is certainly a most useful tool for anyone considering a partnership in the field of writing."

Lillian Brummet
author and radio host, www.brummet.ca

"What a wonderful resource. With so many books now being written by two or more people, *The Collaborator Rules* can help a lot of authors navigate the ins-and-outs, ups-and-downs of working with another strong opinionated individual."

John Kremer
author, *1001 Ways to Market Your Books*

"Sally Shields has written the definitive book on how to play well in the book-writing sandbox. I wish I'd had this book when I was just starting out as a ghostwriter—it would have saved me a lot of angst!"

Alisa Bowman
best-seller and collaborator, *The Skinny*, Broadway 2008

"Funny, smart, a quick read, *The Collaborator Rules* will make you laugh out loud! Sally delivers invaluable information in concentrated sound bites. You can tell she has been media trained well! Anyone who has ever been in a relationship of any kind will benefit from this witty and insightful new gem of an offering."

Wayne Kelly
media trainer, radio host and founder of *www.onairpublicity.com*

The
Collaborator
Rules

101 *Surefire* Ways to Stay Friends with Your Co-Author!

Sally Shields

Safflower Publishing, Inc.
New York, NY

The author represents and warrants that she both owns and has the legal right to publish all material in this book.

Safflower Publishing, Inc.
www.sallyshields.com

ISBN: 978-1-4928-8739-3

PRINTED IN THE UNITED STATES OF AMERICA

This book is dedicated to all collaborators

Contents _____

Acknowledgement _____

A Very Special Thanks to
Asher Brauner

Foreword _____

Writing is a lonely and difficult business. When you're all alone with a computer in the middle of the night and you can't decide if your character should get married or throw herself under a double-decker bus, it would be nice to have someone to ask. When you're pretty sure that what you've just written is either the worst rubbish any mind ever conceived or a stroke of Shakespearian genius, you might feel the need for a second opinion. When you know exactly how the screenplay starts and how it ends but you're missing that teensy part called "the middle," the thought may well cross your mind that what you need is — a collaborator!

Lots of writers work with collaborators. From screenwriting comedy teams to textbook authors, writing is not always best done alone, wallowing in self-pity. And so, many innocent, doe-eyed writers enter into collaboration, without thoroughly considering the consequences of this monumental decision. If your writing is important to you, you must make sure that the collaboration is right for you. And yet, for writers considering collaboration, or already working within that tricky relationship, there has been no recipe for success. There has been no guide that explains everything you should know about collaboration, and more. Until now.

Although the primary focus of this guide is on collaborations between writers, most of the information can also be applied to other types of collaborations and partnerships.

This handbook is designed to take you from your initial desire for a collaborator all the way through every pitfall and every success. The rules for collaboration turn out to be very similar to the basic design for good relationships. That's why this book is set up with a guiding metaphor. Think of yourself as single—or perhaps you're already there. (Perhaps you wish you were, but that's a different story.) This manual takes the bachelor or bachelorette—the solo writer—and leads you from dating (meeting collaborators), to the wedding (who else is invited?), through the honeymoon phase, (working together well), to the sometimes-inevitable divorce (uh-oh).

And it all starts with... *desire*.

PART 1:
Desire Stirs

Rule #1: _____

Realize That Writing is Lonely (That's why God invented coffee shops)

Have you ever had that empty, hollow feeling of working away on a project no one else understands, or shares? Most writers have. Human beings are social creatures. Unless you're a hermit, you like both hearing and talking about your work. It would be lovely to be told that your writing is good, or even that it's interesting. Heck, you'd settle for a chat about the pros and cons of rodent ownership. But there are other ways to solve this problem. You could talk to the walls. Get a dog. Or, better yet, you could get out more. Make a rule for yourself that you will spend at least an hour every day away from your writing, in the company of people. Take a walk in the park, but check the weather first. This is a step many writers forget. Alternatively, go to a coffee shop. Get a latté, and sip it slowly—it's too hot anyway.

Rule #2: _____

Make Sure You're Prepared Emotionally

Before you head into the Land of Collaboration, ask yourself, "Are you sure you're ready for this?" If you're in the middle of a messy divorce, now is not the time to seek out yet another stressful relationship. If you've just fallen head over heels, you don't have the available brain cells to devote to a new collaborator. It is a prerequisite of successful collaboration that you and your collaborator need to be in relatively stable life situations. You should not be on your way to a safari in Kenya, nor moving out of an apartment and constantly changing addresses, and definitely not on your way to the Big House on a two-year bid for embezzling from the 7-11.

Rule #3: _____

Clarify Your Big Idea

Whatever kind of writing you do, whatever size or scope of project you're working on, you need to know what the Big Idea is. Seeking a collaborator when you haven't refined your Big Idea is like shopping for the perfect high-definition TV when you haven't paid the electric bill. If you want to work with someone else, you'll have to be able express your Big Idea clearly and succinctly. "I'm working on a book about music" isn't nearly as helpful as, "I've written the first three chapters of a book about the breakup of the Beatles from Yoko's Ono's artistic point of view. Ultimately, it will be approximately sixteen chapters. The audience is Beatles fans in the U.S." Of course, for that concept you'd need Beatles fans who like Yoko Ono's artistic point of view, and that may not be the biggest demographic...

PART 2:
The Personal Ad

Rule #4: _____

Know How to Write a Personal Ad

No, this doesn't mean you have to go to Match.com and decide if you want tall, dark and handsome or short and stout. But it does mean that you need to ask yourself what you are really after. Define your job, yourself and your need. Do you know what the ideal collaborator would be like? What expertise do they need? What will you provide? What really bugs you? This is a time to be brutally honest with yourself. If you are a good, logical thinker but not the creative type, that's O.K.— now you know what you're missing. If you want to write a comic screenplay but you only have story ideas and no jokes, you know you need Billy Crystal on your side.

Rule #5: _____

Choose Well Early—a Collaborator Who Matches Your Style, or a Slow Descent Into Madness

You may have come across this book and thought, "Hey, I was thinking about a collaborative project. I do need a few tips, but basically this should be a light and entertaining book, because there's not much that can really go wrong." Wrongo, bucko! As will be elaborated in later sections of this guide, the dangers are far worse than you imagine. Brace yourself now. Because if your collaboration goes wrong—and many do—you may end up having given your time, your address, your phone number, and your financial and emotional confidence to a person who not only has stopped working to make things better, but is actively trying to destroy your life. Exaggeration? Not even slightly. If you don't want to risk fans throwing beers at you when you play the outfield, don't take up baseball. And if you don't want to risk vengeful excollaborators spamming your friends with emails defaming you, your family and your life, don't step into the deep pit of collaboration. Consider yourself fairly warned. How can you best avoid all this? Check out the next tip.

Rule #6: _____

Find The Right Person

E ver see one of those successful marriages where the couple is a thousand years old and they are still holding hands like teenagers? Sure, they worked hard on the relationship. But a lot of the reason for their success was the fact that they just met the right person.

Rule #7: _____

Take a Good Look in the Mirror and Stop Flinching

In order to find a good collaborator, you need to think about your weaknesses and quirks. Because if you don't, your collaborator certainly will, sooner or later. So you might as well admit them up front. This doesn't mean that you need to dig into your deepest insecurities or feel awful about past mistakes. It's more a question of style—many difficulties between collaborators come down to not much more than differences in style. Are you a night owl who can't stand early birds? Do you work in brief bursts, or stick to a steady schedule? It's possible to get along with someone who doesn't have the same style as you, but you should be aware of your own patterns and habits and communicate them up front. Maybe your collaborator doesn't mind that you prefer to hum polkas as you work—but it's probably something you should mention if you plan on being in the same room together with this person.

Rule #8: _____

If the Shoe Doesn't Fit, Don't Blame It—Or Your Foot

You may well be one of the great writers of our time. You may be kind to children and small animals—and your collaborator might even be nicer and equally talented. Doesn't that sound like a match made in heaven? Well, not necessarily. You and your potential collaborator may just not be a good fit. It doesn't mean either one of you is to blame. Looking for a great collaborator is like looking for a spouse—you don't need everyone to match, you just need *someone* to match.

Rule #9: _____

Chemistry is Essential

If you've ever been on a failed date, you know that there is no way to overcome an absence of chemistry. Or comfortability. Talk with the other person to see if you're at ease.

Rule #10: _____

Plan a Week of Work in Your Mind Before You Ever Work a Week

Sit down with a calendar and map out your project. When is it due? What are some benchmarks you need to hit along the way? Now think about how many hours you are willing to work each day, each week. Have to drive the kids to soccer practice every day at 3:00? Worth knowing. Don't have a good, quiet place to work? Definitely worth knowing. Because the point of this exercise is to think about the logistics of collaboration, not the art. How many hours a week do you expect the collaborator to work? Which hours? If you live far apart, are you willing to travel, or will you communicate via email?

Rule #11: _____

Your Life Collaborators Are More Important Than Your Work Collaborators

Your friends, your spouse, your family, even your mother-in-law; these are important people in your life (let's hope). If you're going to be spending a lot of time collaborating with someone new, make sure you aren't leaving your existing relationships behind. Another way to think of this is to ask yourself: when I'm done with this project, if I still have a good working relationship but my wife has thrown me out, will I still be happy? (If the answer is yes, you may have bigger concerns than just your writing.) Collaborators certainly can get along with your family—but don't assume it, and don't take the family for granted. Because, really, you don't want your kids asking, "Who is that scary woman who is always sending you emails that make you yell at us?"

Rule #12: _____

You Can Have a Friend, or a Collaborator, But Usually Not Both

Sure, it's tempting. You've got friends who are smart. You know you like each other. Heck, your kids even play in the sandbox together. This could be great—you'll see each other more often than you usually do, so you'll enjoy each other's company more. Right? Wrong. Remember the old adage, "Don't mix business and pleasure?" Collaboration demands a lot out of two people. You will be providing criticism every day. And even if both of you try to do it as nicely as possible, you'll inevitably hurt each other's feelings. And that friend who seems so witty when you see him once every two weeks turns out to be an annoying prankster who doesn't take anything seriously. If you get fed up and end things, you lose a collaborator and a friend—two for the price of one. And your kids will probably be throwing sand in each other's eyes. The only time to collaborate with a friend is when you think the friendship is so strong it can withstand constant mutual criticism and financial strain.

PART 3: Dating

Rule #13: _____

Cast Your Net Wide

Get several recommendations. If you do make up your mind to get help with your project and decide that you'd like a partner, get several references, preferably from reliable, professional sources. Google your prospective co-author's name and all its various combinations. If absolutely nothing comes up, nada, zip, zero, nil, zilch, naught, then Houston, we have a problem. For example, be extra careful if she happens to be your husband's golf-buddy's wife who says that she is a professional writer and editor. Do your background checks—and make it thorough.

Rule #14: _____

Don't Just Bat Your Eyelashes If They Want You

Sometimes, you won't be the person looking for the collaborator—you'll be the one someone else wants. Most of the tips for collaborators still hold true in this situation. Do your research—find out exactly what the person requires. How do they expect the work to proceed? Do they want you to lift the refrigerator while they dust under it? If the project moves along, make sure to protect your legal rights. Get an attorney.

Rule #15: _____

Don't Burn Your Bridges

Sometimes you will be courted, but you know the fit isn't right. Let them down easy. Explain that this project isn't for you, but be nice about it. Keep the door open for future ventures, because even if you won't work with them, they might some day refer you to someone else, and you never know what other endeavors may lead to.

Rule #16: _____

You Might Have to Kiss a Few Frogs Before Finding Your Prince

Suppose you meet someone and decide this might be the collaborator for you. You invite him, he likes the idea. You have a good working meeting, and you see eye-to-eye on what's wrong with the world. Your schedules match wonderfully, and things are going along perfectly. And then your new partner suggests that the financial planning book you're working on ought to be "spiced up with a little hula action." Uh-oh. And you can't talk him out of it. Move on. Try another collaborator. Better to spend eight weeks looking for a collaborator that shares your vision than eight months repairing the damage that the wrong collaborator did to your project, your wallet, and your psyche.

Rule #17: _____

Make Sure That Your Ideas Are At Least In the Same Ballpark

Verify that you and your collaborator are on common ground, and both clearly understand the nature and purpose of the work. Nothing will kill a project quicker than writers who have radically different perspectives. For example, Let's say you want to write a cute little book about how to be a great friend. It might be a warning sign if your collaborator tries to turn it into a theatrical over-the-top satire about the devil incarnate. NEXT.

Rule #18: _____

"Fall in Like" With Your Collaborator

You'll be spending a lot of time together and will have disagreements, so you'd better like him or her and get along well.

Rule #19: _____

Don't Cheat On Your Collaborator

From time to time, both you and your collaborator may have other offers, or want to work with another person. You're a writer and there are a lot of projects in the world. It is only acceptable to accept the other offers if they are for entirely different projects. For example, if your collaborator spends three weeks crafting the perfect balcony scene in your stage play and you decide that you would rather use the advice of some other, different collaborator you've been hiding, guess how well that's going to go over? When to get worried: when your collaborator says, "I'd like to see other people."

(Recognizing Early Warning
Signs)

Rule #20: _____

Check Out How Your Collaborator Gets Along With Others

Remember when you got graded on how well you "played with others" in elementary school? Well, it's even more important for adults. If your potential collaborator complains about an ex-friend that she is still mad at with a vengeance six years later, and then tells you about a falling out she recently had with her babysitter, plus how she hates her sister-in-law, not to mention how her father never spoke to her, and how she can't stand the superficial mothers at her daughter's ballet class, it's a good bet that you will soon be on that list of people!

Rule #21: _____

Beware If Your Collaborator Has Delusions Of Grandeur

E ven if all the above elements fall into place, be wary of someone who promises or is expecting the book to yield great riches, fame, and a slot on Oprah. Thousands of books are published each year, and very few authors achieve that status. The competition is so fierce that even Oprah isn't guaranteed a slot on Oprah. Although your collaborator may have more experience than you, or have some insider publishing knowledge or connections, don't let this intimidate you. If your collaborator were so fabulously knowledgeable and well-connected, she wouldn't be talking to you—she'd be talking to Oprah. Or at least to Dr. Phil. Lessons learned from Freud apply: people brag to compensate for something missing. What is that missing piece for your collaborator?

Rule #22:  _____

If He Wears a Tuxedo To Lunch, Take Heed

If you get an inkling that your potential collaborator's unusual style is way off base from yours, be super aware and don't just brush it off. This could be a sign of her trying to impress you into thinking that she's more professional than she really is. For example, if your potential collaborator suggests a catered poolside meeting when you are just getting together casually, alarm bells should be going off. People don't change very quickly. The way your potential collaborators act in the first days you meet them is a pretty good indication of how they will behave later. In fact, they are probably on their best behavior. In the long run, the fancy luncheon will end up costing you much more than $29.95 and a mimosa headache.

Rule #23: _____

Make Sure Your Collaborator is of Generous Spirit

L et's say you go back to her place after lunch. You've just met, she seems bright and experienced, the sun is shining and the birds are singing. Then she goes to pay her baby-sitter and spends five minutes counting her change to make sure the teenager didn't cheat her out of a dollar. Beep! Beep! Red flag alert! This is just a small microcosm of how she will treat you down the line—and make no mistake, every penny will be accounted for. If you have a different philosophy about money and sharing, beware of this trait.

Rule #24:

Test The Reliability Factor

If your prospective collaborator cancels an appointment to meet you, not once, not twice, but three times in a row, and then tries to cancel a fourth time stating impending rain as the reason for wanting to reschedule, take note and do not expect her to come through for you when the rubber meets the road. Especially if it's a sunny day.

Rule#25: _____

Meet The Parents

If you've seen the movie or experienced the real-life equivalent, you know that an important moment in many relationships is bringing the new person to meet your loved ones. Is this necessary for collaborators? Well, you probably don't want to ask them to eat Mom's meatloaf, and then judge them based on their reaction to that sacred meal. On the other hand, your opinion on the potential success of your collaboration is just that—an opinion. And it's always good to get a second one—or even a third. Set up a casual meeting in which your trusted friends, co-workers or loved ones can meet your potential collaborator. If working long-distance, have your trusted ones review all the emails you've received from her. Your friends may spot things you didn't see, or chose to ignore. Suppose your husband says, "Don't you think it's odd that she is a journalist, yet she doesn't read any newspapers?" This may be a warning sign you missed. Give it the proper weight it deserves. Perhaps ask your would-be collaborator *why* she doesn't read newspapers. And if your co-worker says, "I noticed at lunch that she never asked a single question—she just talked about herself," this is definitely a warning sign. And if you missed it, take another good look.

(The Engagement)

Rule #26: _____

Try a Quick Project Together Before Doing Anything Big

If you or your potential collaborator have a quick job you can work on together, do it first as an audition. This doesn't have to be part of your big project. It might mean sitting together and critiquing the latest article in "Cosmopolitan." Suggest an exercise: "How about we rewrite this thing, just to see if we could make it better?" Make it quite clear that this will help you see how well you work together, and that this is not a paying job. Nor is it intended for publication. You could also offer to help out with something your collaborator is working on. A trial of this sort will be the closest thing to your real work together that you can find. If your collaborator is enthusiastic about the idea, comes up with great concepts, hears and respects your suggestions, adjusts to your schedule as you do to hers, and your little test-project works out well—you may have a winner!

Rule #27: _____

You Don't Have to Get Down On Bended Knee to Ask Nicely

This is the big moment—you've already covered your legal bases, you've had lunch and tried a quick project, you've brainstormed so well you feel like you're Laurel and he's Hardy. Everything seems perfect. But like a shy fiancé, you're not quite sure how to ask. However, since you're going to be working closely together, it's crucial to start this phase of the relationship by being open, honest and above all—yourself. There is nothing wrong with simply asking for what you want. "Would you like to collaborate with me?" will work quite nicely. And supplying a reason always helps. Instead of just, "Wanna work together?" try adding, "It seems like your educational curriculum background is really what this project needs. Would you be willing to work on the project along the lines we've discussed?" Collaborators must feel comfortable in the relationship; that they can be themselves, contribute their unique strengths and even their quirks (which adds spice and flavor) and to fill in each other's gaps. If you get a yes, congratulations! It's a beautiful thing. But no matter how moving the moment is, you probably shouldn't kiss your collaborator.

PART 4:
The Prenup

Rule #28: _____

Put It All In Writing

Well, things look good. You've got a partner and you're getting along. You even admire each other's taste in clothing. You're both ready to work, and you've discussed who will be doing which aspects of the job. You're set, right? WRONG. Until you've got it in writing, nothing has been decided upon. It's time to get your paranoid brain in gear. Imagine that it's one year from now and the person who seems so lovely has suddenly turned into a raging bear. He claims that all the ideas were his in the first place. He says he hasn't written anything in five months because he was only responsible for the introduction. But you don't have any clear evidence of what was agreed to, or maybe you have contradictory emails. This is what professionals call an ungood situation. Now back up in time, take a deep breath, and spell it all out: all the details of who will do what, when, how, where, and for how much. And make it all one document that you both discuss and sign.

Rule #29: _____

Consider Getting it Notarized

ake sure you have a written contractual agreement with each other that records ALL the details, including how you're going to be paid, what happens if one wants out, or if one dies, who's the primary author, timelines for completing the work, whose name appears first, etc. Treat it as a business and protect everyone. And if the involvement of the other person starts to feel less like value-added and more like annoyance, think about breaking the engagement. This way you have an out. Feeling the need for legal advice yet? Try the next tip.

Rule #30: _____

If Your Partner is Insulted When You Hire a Lawyer, Worry

Writing can and should be an art, but it is also a profession. And professionals working on complex projects need to protect their legal rights. Retain your own, separate attorney. Do not give your collaborator the benefit of your lawyer's expertise, as someday, unfortunately, you might have to file a lawsuit against her and your lawyer will not be legally allowed to represent you (as your collaborator could technically claim he represented her as well). How do you explain this to your partner, who might feel you are displaying insufficient trust? Simple. "I always hire an attorney. I recommend you do the same." If your collaborator keeps harping on this issue, maybe there is an ulterior motive.

Rule #31: _____

Remember That There's More to a Book Than a Cover

awyers certainly seem expensive—until you consider the alternative. Without legal protection you might end up in court without a paddle. Remember that novel? The story that was your idea, that you put most of the work into, that opus that has mass appeal and five publishing houses fighting for the rights? Well, that creation somehow became entirely the property of your collaborator, who thought ahead and hired a lawyer when you didn't. Oh, they're making a movie of it? How nice, maybe you can pay ten bucks for admission and twenty for an absolutely gigantic jumbo popcorn, heavily fake-buttered, to shove into your face in misery as the character that was actually based on your life parades across the screen.

Rule #32: _____

... But a Book Does Get Judged By Its Cover!

The reality is that people *do* judge a book by its cover. Don't believe it? Go watch customers in a bookstore for five minutes. They pick up a book—why? Because they are looking at the cover. Then what? They look at the back, to see if Stephen King liked it. Then, most often, they fan the pages, as though they can get a good sense of it by feeling the air it blows out. Discuss with your collaborator what the cover and interior will look like. If necessary, start talking to a design expert. Have a clear picture of what you have in mind for the final product. However, most traditional publishers insist on controlling book cover designs. They may make exceptions for artists or graphic designers, but even then it's rare. Many have their own art departments, special looks and designs and are very proprietary as to how their books should look. That said, developing cover art with your collaborator is wise because it helps give you both the same vision and focus and it can help unify the project. Also it doesn't hurt to let the publisher see your vision because it might inspire or impress—but don't expect them to buy it.

Rule #33: _____

Get a Litigator Who Knows Copyright Law

You know the odd-jobs fix-it guy who hauls your garbage away, helps knock down a wall, and then offers to do your electrical work because he "knows a little bit about it?" If you let him wire your house, prepare for blackouts. It's the same with writing. Don't be tempted a by jack-of-all-trades lawyer who sort of remembers copyright law from law school twelve years ago. You need someone who specializes in the field. And never hire a friend of the family, a distant relative, or an attorney whose concentration is in commercial real estate.

Rule#34: _____

Never Trust Anything To Smiling Handshakes (no matter how much you like your collaborator!)

In other words, don't rely on friendship to carry you through lawsuits. Co-authoring is a HUGE nightmare if one party ends up working harder than the other, or not delivering content promptly, or if your collaborator suddenly does a 180 and ends up boiling a bunny. (For those of you innocent bunnies who were born after 1987, consider adding "Fatal Attraction" to your Netflix queue.)

Rule #35: _____

Always Copyright Your Original Work

If you have a great idea for a project, (or, if you're the one who came up with The BIG IDEA), write it down, work on it as much as you can on your own, and apply for a copyright with the US Copyright office. It doesn't matter how raw a form it's in, this is your brainchild, your hobbyhorse, your magnum opus, your intellectual property, and anything else that comes from it can be labeled a derivative work and will safeguard you from any future parties who may try to claim your efforts as their own. The main points are (1) that ideas can be and are easily stolen and (2) writers must protect themselves. Although you cannot copyright ideas, you can copyright *expressions* of ideas i.e., writings, drawings, musical compositions, etc.—tangible forms or expressions of this nature. So if you have a great idea, write about it and register it for copyright protection. However, someone else can also write about that same idea and register the copyright provided he or she doesn't express it the exact same way you did. As well, copyright exists from the time of its creation, so if you have a great idea and write about it, the time of its conception should be documented on your computer. Then be circumspect; discuss it only with those you completely trust and keep those discussions to the bare minimum until you've reduced it to paper and registered it with the US Copyright Office.

Rule#36: _____

Protect Yourself When Signing a Joint Copyright

If your collaborator wants you to sign a joint-copyright right away, make sure you copyright all original drafts of your work first, and make sure to check "Derivative Work" in sections 6a and 6b on Copyright form TX just in case things take a nosedive (and said collaborator tries to claim your original work as her own later on down the line).

Rule #37: _____

Be Prepared To Be Accused of Copyright Infringement

You've been around a few years, so you probably know that money makes people behave in unexpected and usually unsavory ways. If your collaborator can smell any money to come from your project's future success, chances are the scent will be difficult to resist. Perhaps this is a person who seemed to you to have scruples and ethics. Perhaps this is a person who really nailed that plot difficulty you couldn't seem to solve. How nice. The problem is, this is also a person who is very possibly going to take credit for as much as she can get away with. That includes claiming recognition for as much as the entire work, and accusing you—the one with the original idea—of copyright infringement. This nightmare scenario means you will either have to walk away from the project or spend time, money and energy in court in an attempt to prove your claim. Remedy: copyright all your original work, hire a lawyer before work begins, and document the work you yourself do.

Rule #38: _____

Look Up "Ancillary Rights" on Google

Protecting your copyright means more than just defending your legal rights to publication of the text. Before you get started, try to anticipate all the sources of income. Let's say it's a nonfiction book. You need to secure the rights for publication of the book both domestically and internationally, as well as for any related web sites, and any marketing or merchandising. If there is going to be a little plushy doll that kids buy by the millions, do you really want all that plushy money going to your collaborator, your agent or your publisher—but not to you? As well, think about sequels, branding and trademarks. And work that is related or derived from the original and includes characters or situations which you originated should be yours.

Rule #39: _____

Money Matters

ecide up front if this will be a fifty/fifty split or exactly how you intend to divide up the proceeds. If it is truly equal writing/editing—then split it. If one of you does most of the writing, then make sure that a greater percentage of moneys—whether advance or royalties goes to that person. Also determine what the percentage for future revisions are. For example, if next year the publisher wants you to update certain information, and your collaborator doesn't want to help but you do, how does that effect compensation? All of these things need to be agreed upon before starting.

PART 5:
The Wedding: Who's Invited?

Rule #40: _____

Decide on Justice of the Peace or The Waldorf—Astoria

How you go about working together may have much to do with what kind of publishing you have in mind. If you're going to self-publish, then factor that element into your contract with the other person. If you're aiming for a traditional publisher, then have your agreement with each other reflect that fact. Also, one of you should know how to navigate the waters of royalty houses. And then beware the sharks in those waters.

Rule #41: _____

Be Persistent (but never a pest)

For larger projects such as novels or screenplays, it is always wise to use the services of an established agent. There are many good resources for finding agents, readily accessible in a decent bookstore and online. And the same sources will give you lots of good advice about writing a cover letter, formatting your submission, etc. But all of that is secondary to the main point: your job in this regard is to be as relentless as you need to be. Agents and publishers have more manuscripts than they can handle. So if you believe in your project, you must pursue every available avenue, and then some.

Rule#42: _____

Recognize That Two Halves Make a Whole

This is where having a collaborator may well come in handy. If you are the shy type who has no connections and your collaborator revels in self-promotion and schmoozing, you might want to have your partner work the connections. In other words, one person picks up the other's slack. This does not, repeat, not mean that you should relinquish control. Make sure you keep close tabs on what your collaborator is doing, who has been contacted, what progress has been made with which agent, and so on.

Rule#43: _____

My Agent, or Yours?

Determine who will be the contact with the agent and publisher so neither of them are confused about who to speak with. But make sure that you get a copy of all important data—tell the collaborator and the agent to cc you on everything.

Rule #44: _____

Know Yourself and Stick To Your Guns

If you should be fortunate enough to obtain the services of a competent agent who is excited about your work, do a little dance on the couch. But not for too long—plenty of challenges lie ahead. What you have now is not merely the headache of a two-way collaboration, but a three-way project. Your agent may have expectations you don't want to meet, (The Dreaded Proposal, anyone?), or she might see the project as a comprehensive book when you were thinking of a set of short articles. While you should always listen to advice and remember that professionals know what they're talking about, never lose sight of your own instincts. The agent isn't the writer, and the collaborator doesn't know everything either. While it's good to compromise where appropriate, never bargain away what you truly believe in. If you know, deep inside, that the serial killer nemesis character you created has to be in this book for it to work, don't let anyone tell you otherwise. Meanwhile, make sure that any communication between you or your collaborator with the agent is something all three of you know about. Don't let your collaborator make side deals with the agent, as you could be left on the outside looking in.

Rule #45: _____

Always Make Sure to Set a Deadline That is Comfortable For You (and not just what your collaborator says it should be)

For example, picture a Friday, late afternoon, and you have a three-way conversation with your agent, where it is explained that you need to submit a proposal. Before you can get a word in edgewise, your collaborator announces that she can expect the proposal by the end of the weekend. Who cares if it's your 40th birthday, you have food poisoning, and have two small children to take care of? Speak up, no matter what and insist that you will get back to the agent after you've discussed it privately with your collaborator.

Rule#46: _____

Go to GoDaddy

Most agencies these days insist on a "platform" (i.e. website), so immediately try to procure the domain name of the title of your book, and all its various misspellings. Here's why. Let's say your book is called "The Executioner in Pajamas." Sweet title. Your initial move was to simply nail down the domain name: theexecutionerinpajamas.com. Many moons from now, when your possibly ex-collaborator—or anyone else for that matter—wants to get some of the web traffic that is rightly due you and your book that is flying off the shelves, they might start setting up a web site called www.executionerspajamas.com—or any similar possibilities. Your eager fans will click in the wrong place. That web traffic is gold. Make sure those customers end up on the right web site—yours.

Rule #47: _____

Do Some Planning Before Sitting Down To Write

Clearly define and assign tasks. Be unambiguous about who's doing what. Who's responsible for what portions of the work? Specify in writing exactly how many words each party will contribute and/or allocate specific chapters. Write down any uncertainties and address them one by one and there won't be any surprises.

Rule #48: _____

Have a Clear Outline of Responsibilities and Leadership Roles

Who's going to be the head writer? Decide whether you are writing as equals or if one will be mainly a "line-editor" working with the other person's content, and who has "the final say."

Rule #49: _____

Know That The Top of the Marquee is Better Than The Top of the Mark

Decide whose name comes first WAY before you start the project—and then stick to it, no matter what transpires. The first author is usually considered the lead on an article or work and is reflective of expertise and contribution. If it is a 50/50... then go alphabetical and live with it.

Rule #50: _____

Make Sure the Author's Bios Are About Equal Length (if possible)

If one author is truly more skilled and has more credentials, then so be it. If it's not you, go get more experience. You know you're supposed to anyway ...

Rule#51: _____

Set a Timetable For Completion

$\mathcal{S}$et a schedule, stick to it, and show accountability to your collaborator for delivering work on time.

Rule #52: _____

Realize That it's Called Busy Work for a Reason

Who will apply for the ISBN? Library of Congress number? Planning on using Baker & Taylor, Ingram, or both? (Look these up if you don't know.) How will speaking engagements that result be assigned? (You will probably get calls for speaking as a result of a good book. How will those requests be fulfilled if both parties are speakers?) Will the book be paperback or hard-bound? What about trim size? How many pages? How will you decide on a cover design & graphics?

Rule #53: _____

Ensure That There is Sound Project Management

ecide whether you or your collaborator will take on this responsibility or assign it to someone else. (Writers are not always good managers, so a third-party supervisor can be a good idea). Someone needs to make sure deadlines are met and that both writers have good direction.

Rule#54: _____

Trust is a Two—Way Street

Have a high-confidence, good working relationship before starting the project. Collaborating with an attitude of, "I trust you, my peer," will add value to your writing. Also, your collaborator should be someone who will be truthful about what he or she is thinking and feeling and who will also listen to you. You must offer the same honesty and willingness in return.

Rule#55: _____

Communicate Bad News Nicely

It's been a long day. You've finally finished the research the project needed and you've got an iced tea, possibly Long Island, in hand. You check your email and find that your collaborator has sent you the draft introduction to the book. It doesn't match at all with what you agreed upon, hoped for, or envisioned. In fact, it's so poorly written it reminds you of your own forth-grade science project report— the one with the baking soda volcano. How do you tell your collaborator that you're not exactly pleased? This is where the instructions from the old song come in handy: "Accentuate the positive." Find a way to tell him or her what is good and what is effective, respecting the efforts made. In other words, "You stink" may not be as helpful as, "Here's what I think is working."

Rule #56: _____

Timing is Everything

You have to cut each other a lot of slack and let a lot go (perhaps hold off on criticizing her writing style) when your partner is experiencing difficulties such as health issues, a grieving sister, a father's death, financial pressures, and a mother in the hospital, etc. etc.

Rule #57: _____

Believe It or Not, It Could Be Your Fault

When most folks hear "communication," they think of all the things they want to say. Necessary, sure. But it's also important to listen. Not just spend time on the phone or reading collaborator emails, which you should do, but also actually pay attention. When your collaborator tells you that the metaphor you keep using—"fighting like dogs and mice" isn't really effectual, take note. If you're not sure what's wrong with it, ask a clarifying question.

Rule#58: _____

Be Prepared to Eat Crow

Guess what? Sometimes you make mistakes. Shocking, but true. And certainly not something you want your collaborator to be thinking about too much. But it may well happen that you make a mistake and your cohort turns out to have been right all along. Do you suppose this is a moment when he is going to go out of his way to make you feel better about yourself? Sure, if you happen to be collaborating with the Dalai Lama. In the much more likely event that you are teamed up with an ordinary mortal, get ready. Because what happens next is that your partner will point out in painstaking detail what you did wrong. Even if you already know. Especially if you already know. And the future doesn't look too bright either—the next time a situation like this comes up, he is going to remind you of it and condescendingly suggest that you don't make the same slip-up again. You can't undo the error, but you may be able to stave off much of the future grief if you admit your muddle once, apologize, and listen for a while to what an idiot

73

you are. A little humility goes a long way in a relationship of any sort—your collaborative one included. In other words, own up to what you do and try to make amends. Then you can move on with confidence.

Rule #59: _____

Grandpa May Be Smarter Than You Think

Having a collaborator means that two sets of eyes are looking at the work. That's pretty good—heck, it's double what you had when you were operating alone. But is it enough? It's a good idea early in the process to show your efforts to trusted friends and family, in order to get a wide range of responses. If each of your readers tells you the main character seems unrealistic, it's definitely time to go back to the drawing board. When asking friends to look at your masterpiece, it's important to ask correctly. Emphasize that you don't necessarily want to know if the project is "good," and that you're not simply fishing for compliments. Tell them the objective, then ask them in what ways the writing does or doesn't meet its purpose. For example, if you are writing a series of short stories that is intended to instruct kindergartners in good hygiene (good luck with that), it doesn't help you if your friends tell you they didn't find the stories very interesting. The point is: did my writing achieve my goal?

Rule#60: _____

But If You Do Decide to Run It By Your Best Friend, Keep Your Trap Shut

You can't resist, can you? You've discreetly asked a few acquaintances to comment on the early work, to get some sense of reality. Do not, repeat, *do not* tell your collaborator you've been doing this. It's like waving a red flag in front of a bull. What do you expect your collaborator to say? "Oh, I'm so glad you've let your husband read what I've written so far. It makes me feel special." Or is it more probable to believe that your collaborator is going to feel like you have taken the relationship and stabbed it in the back? How can you know which one is more likely? Well, how would you feel if your collaborator told you that she had spent the weekend sending your manuscript all over the internet just to see what people you have never even met think of it?

Rule #61: _____

Beware: Loose Lips Can Sometimes Sink Ships

You're making good progress on your project. In fact, you just wrote a comic scene that just cracks you and your collaborator up. And it was a sweet piece of collaboration—each of you took the role of one character, and played it out. What a great time to share your joy, huh? No, no, no. While it is useful to have trusted friends and family check your work, particularly in the early going, it is a huge mistake to blab about it. Think of it this way: When Michael Crichton thought of a dinosaur theme park, do you suppose he took out an ad letting the whole city know that he had a great idea, but no book yet? How long would it have been before someone else wrote "Jurassic Park" and beat him to the punch? Don't brag about your tome until it is complete, legally protected, and succeeding. Then, and only then, you might want to buy a cigar, sit back, and soak up the praise.

PART 6:
The Honeymoon Phase

Rule #62: _____

Keep On Talkin'

$\mathcal{A}$ flourishing collaborative relationship is much like a successful marriage in that one of the keys to success is communication. This is easier said than done. It may seem like more work than you're used to doing to call or email your partner once a day, but it will be well worth it. When you're inspired to brainstorm the next scene, and she only wants to talk about the previous one, what do you do? The wrong answer is: ignore your collaborator. Poor communication is probably more likely the cause of grief and disappointment down the road than any other issue between two people.

Acknowledge Your Collaborator's Concerns

Try not to steamroll over your collaborator's anxieties and sensitivities. In other words, steer clear of calling your collaborator "paranoid" even if she asks to you to fax her a copy of the joint-copyright that you filled out last week, as she is suspicious that you may have purposely left her name off of it.

Rule#64: _____

Try Not to Jump to Conclusions

In other words, give your collaborator the benefit of the doubt. Don't just make assumptions about what you think she means. Ask her for clarification.

Rule #65: _____

Be Prepared for Lots of Give & Take

This does not mean, "You give, I take."

Rule #66: _____

Try Not to Be Passive Aggressive

Picture yourself having the following conversation with your collaborator:

You: "Some of the things that you've been doing with the Sally character are ... interesting."
Collab: "What do you mean by interesting?"
You: "Oh, it's probably not important..."
Collab: "Wait, what? What is it?"
You: "I mean, it's just a book. It's not that big a deal. How's your grandpa?"
Collab: "What are you saying? Should I delete Sally?"
You: "If you think you want to do something like that, who am I to stop you?"

In other words: ick. Got something on your mind? Say it directly, but politely.

Rule #67: _____

Don't Treat Your Collaborator Like Your Parent, Child, or Paid Employee

Blithely instructing your collaborator to grab muffins on the way to the meeting is a good way to get a muffin thrown at your head.

Rule #68: _____

Even When You Don't Agree, Offer Your Support

When your collaborator suggests a direction for the project that you think is wrong, don't tell her she's wide of the mark. Tell her how you see it, why you see it that way, and let it sit a while. And do not forget that this is the perfect moment to tell her how much you appreciate whatever it is you might appreciate about her: her hard work, her cheerful personality, her cunning way with prepositions. Because even if being nice wasn't its own reward, it is also the case that this is the person you are going to want support from in the future.

Rule #69: _____

Be Prepared to Make Compromises—And Lots Of Them

It's just not human nature that you and your collaborator will always agree. You will have to take your beloved ideas and style and worldview and actually modify them to fit with another person. That's right, compromise. You will have to do that or you will be working alone real fast. Compromise is part of being in any kind of couple. Accept that. Right now. Stop reading this for a moment, take a deep breath, close your eyes if you're feeling secure enough. You can even put the book down, but pick it right back up. O.K., have you accepted that? Now, we can move on.

Rule #70: _____

Return Your Collaborator's Phone Calls in a Timely Manner

You don't have to jump whenever your partner leaves a message, but you really ought to respond the same day. And from your point of view, let your collaborator know when you feel communication is inadequate. If you've been waiting for more than three days for a response to your key question, you're waiting too long. As in a marriage, balance is key. No one wants to be bothered constantly, but no one wants to be ignored, either. Talk about talking with your collaborator, express what your expectations and frustrations are. Prepare to spend a lot of time communicating in one way or another with your collaborator. If the thought of that spooks you, consider getting out of the project.

Rule #71: _____

Strive to Spell Your Collaborator's Name Correctly

Seems obvious, doesn't it? And you do know how to spell his name. But then one day you get it wrong. Well, it turns out this is a pet peeve of his. Didn't know that, did you? Well, now you've got to hear about your carelessness, or apologize profusely, or be doomed to a sense of disappointment and disgust vectoring in your general direction. And whatever you do, get the name right next time. You're not allowed to make this particular mistake again for the next one hundred years, however the heck it's spelled.

Rule #72: _____

... And Try Not to Name Call

... and by all means don't use facetious names like "Chickie" lest your collaborator has some deep psychological aversion to the hypocorism that you had no prior knowledge of, and you inadvertently end up stepping on a land-mine! Avoid this pitfall by sticking to your collaborator's Christian name at all times, even when he's behaving in ways Christ would not approve of.

Rule #73: _____

Beware Those Digital Dangers

A long time ago, there was a system of communication in which human beings would get in the same place and speak in such a way that they could hear each other directly. True story! Then Albert Einstein or Marie Curie or one of those smart inventor types (Edison?) came up with a new tool. It was called a "telephone." Now, people could talk to each other without leaving home, and without having to smell each other's cooking! Later, of course, Al Gore invented the Internet, and everyone started sending emails. You don't have to see anyone, you don't have to talk to them. It's perfect, right? LOL! However, one of the great dangers of email is that it's too fast. Case in point: you read a message from your collaborator suggesting you revise the third chapter. You, on the other hand, think it's a masterpiece. Also, the third section is in your area of expertise and your collaborator knows nothing about it. Not only that, but you stipulated in your original written scope of work that the third episode was solely your responsibility. So you fire off an email: "3rd. chap fine, leave it." Guess how much respect your collaborator feels from this missive? Guess how nicely she feels about it. Maybe you meant it in funny way, so you added a smiley. Think that caused her to grin? Think again. Once the context of full human communiqué is stripped away, meaning is lost. You have to go out of your way out to explain what you mean, to imagine yourself receiving the email. Is it truly clear? Is it respectful?

Rule #74: _____

Get Microsoft Word for Dummies

It might come in handy when your collaborator asks you to fix the spacing and remove the extraneous periods in the glossary section. (Know how to save a word doc, anyone?)

Rule#75: _____

Make Sure You Have a System for Co-Editing a Project

For example, it is not a good idea to work from too many versions at once because then things get unwieldy. Check out GoogleDocs! You can highlight your changes in red, orange or yellow. Or fuscia. Or magenta. Or cyan. Agree on the process. Define who has the final say on the revisions in question, or who has veto power. i.e. One co-author always has the right to refuse what the other co-author has written if they disagree with it. Kind of like the Beatles' approach to song-writing, if you believe them! Also, make sure you consent to have the book be professionally edited by a third party when all is said and done. Oh, and rule of thumb: good idea to label things.

Rule #76: _____

Try to Establish One "Voice" Throughout

L et's suppose the first sentence of your book is: "Times wuz tough on the ol' prairie but we wuz together." And the second sentence is: "Glaringly, our familial unit was ensconced within a vale of undereducated ruffians, and Mother fainted once a day, as if upon schedule." Kinda jarring for your reader, no? Sometimes editors rewrite your stuff anyway, to meld styles, so this may be a moot point! However, determine in advance who will handle the alterations when it comes back from the publisher's copy editor.

Rule #77: _____

Be Fair

If you want to cut something, be open to your collaborator's suggestions for cutting things as well. If you want to add an afterword, then maybe your collaborator's preface isn't such a bad idea.

Rule#78: _____

Beware of Emails That Pass in the Night

Imagine you are collaborating online and you've written a question to your collaborator. The next day you receive a response that has nothing do with your message. Frustrated yet? If not, repeat cycle until thoroughly dissatisfied. Or, try picking up the phone.

Rule#79: _____

Avoid Using All Caps When Emailing Your Collaborator

She will think you are yelling at her. Maybe you are, but AVOID caps anyways.

Rule #80: _____

Be Very Patient With Your Collaborator

Let's say you've been providing your readers with a constant stream of useful information via your web page. You've got some avid fans and you'd like to be able to post blogs or questions and answers on a weekly basis. But you've been relying on the web designer. Then, one day, in an effort to be cutting edge, you tell your collaborator about your discovery: a function called an Admin Page, which allows you to change the content of the website with a username or password, all without having to bother the computer guy. But your collaborator doesn't get it. She thinks a sophisticated use of a computer is knowing how to Google "Harry Potter." Try to be as gentle as possible. Think of her like an elderly aunt, and refrain from showing frustration if she doesn't understand. After all, there may well be something out there that you don't understand— unlikely, but possible.

Rule#81:  _____

Explain it Again. And Again. And Again. And Again.

It's clear in your mind: the travel guide you're writing is about the U.S., but it is intended for the European market. And yet that fellow voyager of yours, the collaborator, keeps putting in references that only Americans would get. She describes Boston as, "Like San Francisco, but without Newsom." You point out this might be a little difficult for the average Italian traveler. So she rewrites it. This time she calls Boston, "A nice break from all that red-state Nascar crowd." Hmm. Should you let it go, or should you explain it again? And again...

Rule #82: _____

Share the Wealth

No, not that wealth. Always keep your collaborator in mind when you find good resources. For example, if you've located a web site that gives tips that are useful for your research, let your partner know. If you are planning to interview someone important, either find a way for both of you to be there to ask questions, or tape it so your collaborator can use it too. If you bought a good agent book, it's not just yours.

Rule#83: _____

Celebrate Your Milestones

This is more important than you may think. If you've done writing of any length, you know that clear moments of achievement and closure are rare. Much more common is the ongoing project that never seems to be going anywhere until one day it sort of flops down, nearly dead of exhaustion, and you decide to just print and staple in order to put it out of its misery. Before that happens, take care of yourself and your collaborator. Go out for a lunch of moderate size if you finish a chapter, and if you finish a section, you're entitled to dinner at a nice restaurant.

Rule #84: _____

What to Expect When You (and Your Collaborator) are Expecting

So, you and your collaborator have actually succeeded, and created a work of art. The hard part is done; the book is finished, right? WRONG! Now you must step into the world of book marketing. Because no matter how famous or high-profile your publishing company is, you are still going to be expected to promote your own work (that is, unless you're Stephen King or Deepak Chopra, or some weird hybrid stepchild of the two). Customers have tens of thousands of new books to choose from every month. Why should they choose yours? Most often, the answer isn't just the quality of the book. The answer is the marketing. That's what the big publishing houses really do—set their books up with good marketing. You must now go back to the drawing board with your collaborator, and have a Clear Outline of Responsibilities and Leadership Roles. Put in writing who is expected to do what and when. It might work out great if one of you is a homebody and decides to do radio and blog tours from the comfort of your home office, while the other goes on the road promoting to bookstores across America. But again, it could open up a whole other can of worms, a Pandora's Box, so to speak, if one collaborator feels that they are doing the lion's share of the work, or most of the heavy lifting. (If you feel the preceding sentence mixed too many metaphors, see Rule #55: Communicate Bad News Nicely.)

Rule #85: _____

Lean on Each Other

It's nice to be able to commiserate with someone that understands how you feel, especially when the rejections start coming in. And make no mistake—you'll get plenty of them, no matter how good you think your work is!

PART 7:
Trouble in Paradise

Rule #86: _____

If You Don't Work in a Church, Don't Expect Miracles

*A*las, not all goes well all the time. Aristotle said that we can't really appreciate happiness unless we have unhappiness, and maybe that's true. But for many reasons, your collaborative honeymoon has come to an end. Maybe it was fated to—after all, honeymoons don't last forever. And it's most likely that you got along during the early going, because that initial burst of creativity overcame any incipient personality conflicts. But now it's time for the long slog of a marriage. And the successful partnerships that last past the celebratory phase do so because both spouses accept that the bloom is off the rose, but there is still enough good to salvage. If your collaborator is starting to get on your nerves, it's time to accept that irritation, work around it, or resolve it. Because you don't want to end it if it's mostly a positive thing. That's why most of the tips in this section are designed to help you work around the difficult spots. There is nothing so problematical between two individuals who want the same things that can't be solved with dialogue, inquiry, learning the other's POV, history, and time. Don't let your pride get in the way—it's one of the seven deadly sins.

Rule #87: _____

When Her Dog Dies, Send Her a Fruit Basket

... or you may be accused of being an insensitive jerk. O.K., you never met the dog. In fact, you didn't even know she had a dog. And when she told you, you made the mistake of saying you were sorry to hear it—and moved on. Wrong! Fruit basket, flowers, something. We are in mourning.

Rule #88: _____

Beware Of Using Clichés

Try not to describe your collaborator's work in clichés such as, "runaway train" even if she uses the term, "flesh-eating dragon" to describe your mother-in-law, or say, "You dangled the carrot!" when she reverts back to a pre-edited version of something you just couldn't live with. Especially do not declare, "You created a monster!" when describing how it was she who actually encouraged you to trust your instincts. In fact, it's probably best to leave monsters entirely out of any conversations with collaborators.

Rule #89: _____

Know That Your Collaborator May Have Selective Hearing

You: "I like the way you put an orphanage in the background as the train goes by. But I think the character could use an overhaul. She's morphed into a whiny ten-year-old and we had originally envisioned a garrulous crone. I really feel we need to be true to our original vision."

Your collaborator: "Cool! I can expand the orphanage. I know a lot about orphans—I did some research when I played "Annie" in Jr. High. Hey! We could have it be a musical!"

Rule #90: _____

Try Not to Blow Things Out of Proportion

Failure to spell "necessary" correctly three times in a row does not actually mean that he "doesn't even care about this project."

Rule #91: _____

Get A Hold of Your Highly Reactive Hysteria

If you're saying right about now, "WHAT the !@%^&*!!!? ME?!!! I don't have highly reactive hysteria!!!!" then no more needs to be said.

Rule #92: _____

Never Threaten to Break a Contract

It's legally problematic, bad manners, and a very effective way to destroy all good will between you and the people you are supposedly working with. While you're at it, avoid threatening in general. (Or threatening generals.)

Rule #93: _____

Blocking Communication is a Very Bad Idea

Remember when you were six years old and you wanted to scream, "*MOM!!!*" because your older brother was holding your arm behind your back so high up you could scratch your forehead? And recall how he then clamped his other hand over your mouth, practically ending your short life? And recollect how you tried to bite his hand, but he cleverly kept adjusting the angle so that the worst you could do was make his hand disgustingly wet? Don't put your hand over your collaborator's mouth, or try to block any communication. You'll just get a wet hand. Eww.

Rule#94: _____

Consider that Your Collaborator's Opinion is Valid, and Don't Be Disrespectful

... even if you're beginning to get the sense that your collaborator may be crazy as a soup sandwich. (Twilight Zone, anyone?)

Rule #95: _____

Never, Ever, Invite Third Parties to Mediate If You're Having Problems Unless They're Professionals

(i.e. Don't have your spouse call your collaborator and yell at her.)

PART 8:
Divorce

Breaking Up is Hard to Do
(but necessary sometimes)

Rule #96: _____

Don't Be Surprised If You Lose Interest in the Project

It seemed like a good idea about ten thousand years ago. Then the work started, and the collaboration started off on an odd note, then you had to slow down because your collaborator contracted a tropical ailment despite residing in Ypsilanti, Michigan, then there were the endless emails that said nothing, then you had to sit down day after day to a joy that had become a job. Is it any wonder you're getting wanderlust?

Rule #97: _____

Have the Guts to Call it Off ('cause when it's over, it's over)

reaking up is hard to do, but staying together may be worse. Is the collaboration costing you more time, headache, and energy than it's worth? Are the results worse than you could do on your own? It may be time to make that call you've been dreading.

A Quick Guide to Stalkers (and Other Bizarre Collaborator Behavior)

Rule #98: _____

Expect the Unexpected

E xpect that your ex-collaborator may get paranoid, and send you threatening lawyers letters warning you that if you are to use any of her material you will be prosecuted to the full extent of the law and thrown in jail until kingdom come and have all your extremities amputated and you will be hung from your neck in a dungeon with no food, water or sunlight ... or cable TV.

Rule#99: _____

If All Else Fails, Practice Voodoo

If you feel as if your former collaborator has put a curse on you, hire a shaman. Try the Yellow Pages under, "Exorcism: Literary."

The Next Relationship: Collaborating on the Rebound, or Enjoying the Singles Scene?

Rule #100: _____

Consider Work for Hire

If you still feel the need for a collaborator, perhaps you should consider hiring someone on Elance or Craigslist, and simply pay for their services. Just take care to find out what your bidder desires or expects in terms of recognition. Will he get author credits or a simple mention on the acknowledgements page? Will he be doing light editing, or most of the heavy lifting? Make sure that he's okay with whatever you decide before you begin the process.

Rule #101: _____

Try Flying Solo; As Ultimately, You Are Your Own Best Collaborator

You have felt the frustration of doubting the quality of your writing. You recognize your own weaknesses and you can tell someone else could probably fill in the gap pretty well. Wait. Before you take the jump into collaborating again, remember what a great collaborator with yourself you were before this all started. To review: You are always there whenever you're there, you won't ever sue yourself for copyright infringement, you communicate instantly and constantly with yourself, you don't talk too loudly or have an odd odor about you. That's a lot—are you sure you need more? Oh, and you may be a bit of a dictator and be happier having total control. Food for thought. And now that you have collaborated, no matter how well it went, you are wiser for the wear. As the divorce is finalizing and the custody issues are being ironed out, this is no time to decide what to do next. Take a little time off, think about what happened, enjoy your actual life, spend some quality time with your sweaty personal trainer, and in a few months, you'll know whether you're ready again. When you are, open this manual up at page uno.

Final Thoughts _____

Not everyone has to write. It is a choice. For some, it is a creative drive. For others, it is a profession that fits their skills. And as you most likely know, it is a line of work in which substantial rewards are scarce. Rarer still are projects that yield tangible and artistic results. In other words, if you don't love it, don't do it.

As with most of life's complexities, the best thing about working with a collaborator is also the worst. It is the fact that another human being is involved alongside you in one of the most important, most heartfelt endeavors you can undertake. When that collaborator disappoints, upsets, or angers you, it can be one of life's great frustrations. Much of this guide is meant to help you protect yourself in such situations, but there is little that can shield you from suffering emotionally when your partner is being a jerk.

On the other hand, collaborating can also be the most wonderful thing that ever happened to your project, and maybe even to you. Constructing a brand-new creation and sending it out into the world can be a magnificent experience. When it succeeds on financial or artistic merits, when you feel proud of it, sharing that pride is a fantastic feeling that may just make all those sleepless nights and endless emails worth it.

Love,
Sally Shields

The Instant Collaborator Solutions Worksheet

Here is an easy four-step worksheet to help you apply *The Collaborator Rules* to your own particular collaborative situation. The fundamental idea is to jot down all the things that you do that seem to bother your collaborator (and all the things that your collaborator does that bother you) and what was said at those times. You will then come up with a rule title and a solution to deal with each and every troublesome circumstance that arises. This handy mnemonic will help you remember how to do this:

I — Identify the problem

N — Note what was said

C — Create a rule

S — Set up a solution

Identify the problem. In other words, tell your story (i.e. What happened, what you did, what she did)

Note what was said (i.e., what you said, what he said, exact quotes are good here)

Create a rule title. Here are some examples of the ways that you might begin this phrase:

Realize That, Make Sure, Clarify, Know That, Know How To, Try to, Try Not to, Find, Take, Don't Blame, Don't Just, Don't Burn, Expect, Don't expect, Don't Be, Plan, Cast, Get, Give, When, Check Out, Beware If, Beware of, Take Heed, Test, Meet, Ask, Put, Consider, Consider that, Remember That, Recognize That, Ensure That, Worry When, Always, Never, Strive to, Be Prepared to, Be Prepared for, Protect, Look Up, Decide On, Stick to, Go to, Do Some, Have a, Set, Communicate, But if, Keep on, Acknowledge, Offer, Return, Get, Avoid, Explain, Share, Celebrate, Lean, etc.

Set up a solution

Formulate your resolution. The objective is to always give your collaborator the benefit of the doubt at this point in the process. This comes under the umbrella of good will. However, be aware that you may have to stick to your guns at times. Although compromise is key, ultimately you should trust your instincts and do what ever it is that you feel you need to do for the sake of the project. This comes under the umbrella of self-preservation!

I.N.C.S. for T.I.C.S.

Remember, you won't be able to prevent perplexing collaborator comments and confusions overnight. This is a system that must be developed over time. The trick is to realize that once you have identified a certain area of conflict between you and your collaborator, it is likely that the very same situation will surface again. (After all, how many times have you had the same old argument with your spouse about something, right?) The goal is to prevent you from having the same old reactions to repeat misunderstandings, by using **T**he **I**nstant **C**ollaborator **S**olutions (**T.I.C.S.**). Eventually you will create your own personalized set of rules customized for your very own collaborator. This is your ace-in-the hole because you will then be prepared the NEXT time a similar circumstance occurs. Ultimately, your collaborator will be hard-pressed to find anything to complain about (and you might be pleasantly surprised on your end as well). You will begin to coexist peacefully, create abundantly, and experience smooth sailing. It's fun once you get the hang of it, and you will be delighted when you develop a genuine mutual admiration society with one-another—and hopefully you will have created a life-long friendship in the process.

Enjoy!

About the Author _____

Sally Shields is an award-winning pianist, composer, speaker, author and radio personality. Co-host of the exciting new BlogTalkRadio show, "Blurb!" Shields has been featured in *Star Magazine*, *Obvious*, *My Day*, *Girlfriendz*, *For the Bride* and many others. Endorsed by Dr. Laura Schlessinger and Martha Stewart, she has appeared on Fox and Friends, Rachel Ray, Tyra Banks, and the nationally syndicated *The Daily Buzz* with her #1 Amazon.com bestseller, *THE DAUGHTER-IN-LAW RULES!* Winner of the 17th annual Great American Jazz Piano Competition, her book, *Modern Jazz Piano,* is the standard theory manual for several music programs, including Princeton University. She performs worldwide, and her music is currently featured on the ABC TV daytime drama *All My Children.* When not traveling and performing around the world—Sally lives in New York City with her husband and their two children.

Please visit Sally on the web at www.sallyshields.com for contest giveaways, free bonus gifts, Sally's newsletter, 101 Ways to market your book, product or service, free music, ... *and more*!

Also Available from Sally Shields

○ **Sally's Self-Publishing & Bestseller 101 Coaching Program**

You've got a great idea for a book, or you've already written one. You may have even self-published and have a few hundred of them boxed up in your basement or garage. You've given away a few copies to your family and friends. Very nice. Now what?

Sally comes to the rescue with delightful and witty ways to sell a LOT of books, through fun PR strategies! If you're ready to reach more readers with your message and your book, this may be just the information you have been looking for.

Please visit: www.sallyshields.com/coaching for more information

○ **Publicity Secrets Revealed! (What every PR firm *doesn't* want you to know!)**

This guide includes:

✓ how to create a killer media release that will have radio hosts clamoring to interview you

✓ sample press release templates

✓ what every author needs on their website

✓ 7 hook strategies guaranteed to get you publicity

✓ how to get corporations to purchase your book in bulk

✓ how to get your book into Wal-Mart

✓ sample cover letters, sales sheets order forms and printer quote info

✓ how to prepare a corporate sponsorship proposal

✓ sample PPT presentation that can earn you up $150,000

... and much, *much* more!

Please visit: www.sallyshields.com/psr for more information.

As well: _____

- ○ Private Consultations
- ○ Sally Shield's Newsletter
- ○ Speaking Engagements
- ○ Sally Shields Gift Certificates
- ○ *The Collaborator Rules* E-book
- ○ The Self-Publishing & Best Seller101 Workshop
- ○ Publicity Secrets Revealed! Home Study System

Every bit of Sally's philosophy is designed to make a profound and positive improvement in your life, intensify your level of happiness and help you live far more peacefully with your collaborator!

Please visit Sally on the web at www.sallyshields.com for contests, giveaways, free bonus gifts, Sally's newsletter, the 101 *Surefire* Ways to Market Your Book, Product or Service, free music ...*and more!*

Note: This book helps raise money for the Make a Wish Foundation. Since 1980, the Make-A-Wish Foundation® has enriched the lives of children with life-threatening medical conditions through its wish-granting work. Since its humble beginnings, the organization has blossomed into a worldwide phenomenon, reaching more than 167,000 children around the world. A network of nearly 25,000 volunteers serve as wish granters, fundraisers, special events assistants and in numerous other capacities. For more info, please visit: Wish.org.

ATTENTION: SCHOOLS AND CORPORATIONS

THE COLLABORATOR RULES is available at quantity discounts with bulk purchase for educational, business, or sales promotional use. For information, please contact: SPECIAL SALES DEPARTMENT, 324 WEST 263rd STREET, NEW YORK, NY 10417 or email sally@theDILRules.com or phone (718) 543-5524.

www.ingramcontent.com/pod-product-compliance
Lightning Source LLC
Chambersburg PA
CBHW051313170526
45166CB00002B/529